YOUR KNOWLEDGE HAS VALUE

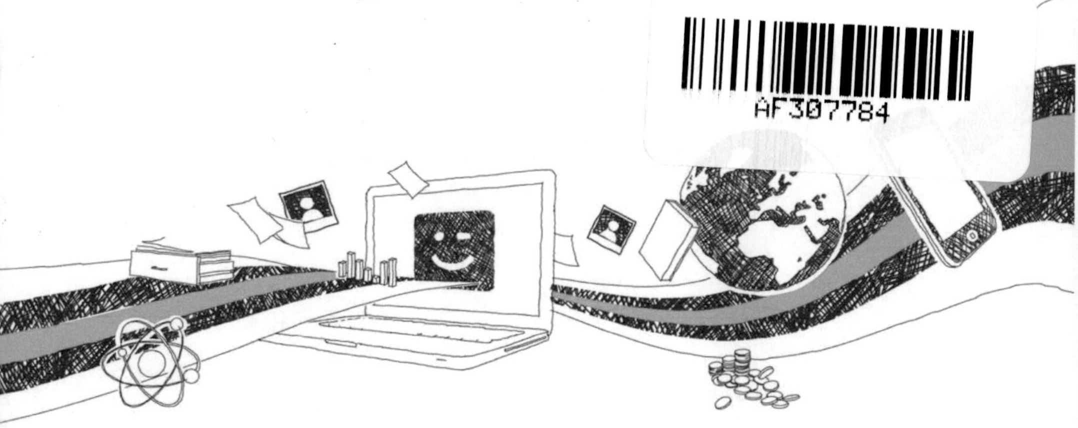

- We will publish your bachelor's and master's thesis, essays and papers

- Your own eBook and book - sold worldwide in all relevant shops

- Earn money with each sale

Upload your text at www.GRIN.com and publish for free

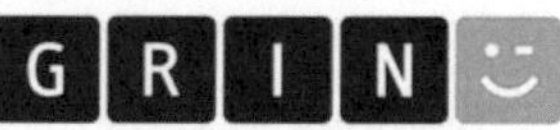

Bibliographic information published by the German National Library:

The German National Library lists this publication in the National Bibliography; detailed bibliographic data are available on the Internet at http://dnb.dnb.de .

Imprint:

Copyright © 2016 GRIN Verlag
Print and binding: Books on Demand GmbH, Norderstedt Germany
ISBN: 9783668485341

This book at GRIN:

https://www.grin.com/document/370263

Christina Haupt

George Catlin's Portraits of Native Americans

Visual Means to Memorialize the Subject

GRIN Verlag

University College Cork

History of Art

George Catlin's Portraits of Native Americans:
Visual Means to Memorialize the Subject

Essay

HA 2009: Creator and Subject:

Themes in Portraiture

Autumn Semester 2016

Christina Haupt

Visiting EU Student

Date of Submission: 09.11.2016

<u>Introduction</u>

'Our Indian life, I know, is gone forever.'[1]

These words from a member of the Hidatsa tribe express the feeling which arose in the early 19th century in the United States. The belief that Native American life had no future was initially promoted by white settlers of the *New World* and encouraged artists like George Catlin to memorialize some of the remaining Native American people in portraits. This essay will critically analyse the painter's use of visual means to represent the subject and demonstrate that Catlin did not depict his sitters entirely lifelike by focusing on the authenticity, modifications and external influences of his portraits. The brief historical and cultural contextualisation of the topic will be followed by an analysis of the portraits of the tribal chiefs Stu-mick-o-súcks and Máh-to-tóh-pa as examples of 'Republican Indians'. Subsequently, I will scrutinize the historical impact of the artist's portraits by introducing Catlin's narrative portrait of Wi-jún-jon, which documents an Indian individual's fate and reveals the artist's attitude towards Native Americans' encounter with civilisation.

Especially Truettner's book "Painting Indians and Building Empires in North America 1710-1840" and the "Letters and Notes" of Catlin were of great use during my research.

<u>Relevant Background</u>

The historical and cultural circumstances in which Catlin's portraits of Native Americans are embedded is essential for their interpretation.

The United States of the early 19th century is characterised by persisting tensions between settlers and indigenous tribes. The belief that 'savages' needed to be 'civilized' and the myth of 'Manifest Destiny' were used to excuse the ferocious westward movement of the white population.[2] Simultaneously, the government advertised ideas of the 'Republican Indian' with noble virtues, whose extinction was inevitable.[3] This nostalgic attitude towards Native Americans had a significant impact on artists such as George Catlin, who spent several years peacefully encountering indigenous tribes in order to paint their representatives individually. Thus, he understood it as his mission

---

[1] Waheenee (Hidatsa), in: *The Wisdom of the Native Americans*, ed. Nerburn, K., Novato, 1999, 55.
[2] Pohl, F., 'Old World, New World: the Encounter of Cultures on the American Frontier', in: S. Eisenman, *Nineteenth Century Art; A Critical History*. London, 1994, 145.
[3] Truettner, William H. *Painting Indians and Building Empires in North America 1710-1840*. California, 2010, 16f.

to '[fly] for their rescue – not of their lives or of their race (for they are "*doomed*" and must perish), but to the rescue of their looks and modes'.[4] Consequently, his artworks need to be filtered through their ideological background and read as documents of their *Zeitgeist*.

Stu-mick-o-súcks (Buffalo Bull's Back Fat)

One of the best examples of a 'Republican Indian' and the political influence in Catlin's work is the portrait of Stu-mick-o-súcks (Fig. 1). The Blackfoot chief's authority is underlined by the portrait-genre itself, which was traditionally associated with statesmen. Although these portraits appreciated realism, they were manipulated to serve a certain class or ethnical ideal.[5] Bearing in mind that the artist had connections to Federalists, a sachem represents virtues and hierarchical order suitable for Republican ideology.[6] In combination with the romanticising of Native American life, Catlin depicts one of the last representatives of 'noble races of red men'.[7]

This nobility is described in Catlin's letter, when he introduces Stu-mick-o-sucks as 'a good-looking, dignified Indian, about fifty years of age, and superbly dressed'.[8] The strong facial features and the chief's calm, direct gaze underline his intellectuality. According to Catlin, the remarkable hairstyle identifies Stu-mick-o-súcks as a member of his tribe and the proud display of his long hair reveals him as a successful warrior.[9] This statement is supported by the vast amount of scalp-locks, which are used as battle-trophies to decorate the sachem's leather tunic and which caught Catlin's special fascination.[10]

Thus, the reader gets the impression that the artist had carefully studied his subject's costume in connection to tribal customs before portraying him as lifelike. Nevertheless, the comparison between Catlin's original sketch (Fig. 2) and the later painting reveals significant manipulations in the depiction of Stu-mick-o-sucks. While the half-length drawing shows the chief seated in front of painted indigenous tepees, the environment is omitted in the later three-quarters portrait. Consequently, the focus is

---

[4] Catlin, G., 'Letter-No. 2', in *Letters and Notes on the North American Indians.*, Vol. I, Massachusetts, 1995, 17.
[5] Groseclose, B., *Nineteenth-Century American Art.* Oxford, 2000, 36 – 41.
[6] Truettner, 65f.
[7] Catlin, 'Letter No. 2', 17.
[8] Ibid., 33.
[9] Ibid., 58
[10] Ibid., 33-35.

laid on the subject's serious expression, which suggests authority and intelligence. This representation was commonly used in heroic portraiture to convey the impression of power.[11] Interestingly, the artist added a feather headdress and face painting to emphasise and affirm the wide-spread idea of 'Indianness'.[12] The initial pipe cannot be recognized as such and thus turns into an indefinable mystic object. Therefore, Catlin consciously diminishes realistic likeness by the visual language of his time to contribute to the impression of an 'exotic other'. He makes historical references to 'an appearance purely classic' to convey an 'authentic' image of Indian nobility.[13]Yet, he is simultaneously underlining characteristic features of the depicted individual.

Máh-to-tóh-pa (Four Bears)

To get a deeper understanding of how George Catlin represents Native Americans characteristically it is important to introduce another portrait. Máh-to-tóh-pa was considered a welcoming Native American and thus became subject of two of Catlin's and other artists' paintings. George Catlin seems impressed by the second chief of the Mandan tribe at their encounter, when he describes him as the 'most popular man in the nation. Free, generous, elegant' and 'the most extraordinary man […] of Nature's noblemen'[14]. The tribal and individual characteristics of Máh-to-tóh-pa are clearly visible in the 1932 half-length portrait (Fig. 3), which depicts him in ¾-profile to stress the strong indigenous features. The naked tanned upper-body is placed before an undefined smooth grey-greenish background. The Native American's skin is partially painted with assumingly red earth and covered with battle scars. The leather blanket on his lap is decorated with numerous scalp-locks to underline his victories. The second chief's hairstyle is typically Mandan, for the long hair is 'divided into plates or slabs […] and filled with […] glue and red earth'[15]. The visual emphasis on the special hairstyle is surely a demonstration of tribal pride; but it also marks the painter's fascination for this custom. Therefore, the half-length portrait provides an authentic and highly realistic image of Máh-to-tóh-pa, although it is adapting to established visual patterns concerning the portrait-genre in order to convey the sitter's status.

---

[11] Knowles, S., 'Lecture 1: 'Introduction', in: *Creator and Subject*, UCC, 16.09.16.
[12] Truettner, 90.
[13] Catlin, 'Letter No. 5', 36.
[14] Catlin, 'Letter No. 13', 104.
[15] Ibid., 107.

The same subject is treated slightly differently in Catlin's full-length portrait (Fig. 4). Máh-to-tóh-pa appears to be standing in full indigenous costume on a grass plain with discreetly painted bushes or trees in the greyish background. Again, he is presented in ¾-profile and as a clearly noticeable a person of tribal authority. The scalp-locks on the arms of the knee-long tunic and leggings indicate success on the battleground. The impressive horned headgear and the floor-length feather headdress contribute to the impression of power. Truettner suggests that the second chief of the Mandan tribe used his meetings with artists as opportunities to influence the painting by choosing specific outfits and attributes for each sitting.[16] Nevertheless, the artist did not depict Máh-to-tóh-pa completely as he wished to be remembered, but chose to manipulate the painting strongly in order to maintain the contemporary image of a dignified, once powerful warrior.[17]

It follows that Catlin's representations of Native Americans were influenced by both, the subject and the creator, as well as the mood of its time.

Didactic Portraits: *Wi-jún-jon (Pigeon's Egg Head, The Light)*

George Catlin's portraits are not only subjected to the depictions of sachems and tribal authorities, but also cover a wide range of portraits of women, children, warriors and medicine-men. Some of Catlin's paintings have a didactic purpose, such as the portrait of the ball-player Tullock-cish-ko in his playing costume and equipment, which serves to illustrate the artist's explanation of the tribal game.[18] Furthermore, he painted a very significant portrait of Wi-jún-jon (Fig. 5) between 1837 and 1839, representing a travelled Native American on his arrival and his return from the Western civilization.

The paintings discussed previously presuppose that the sitter is a pure Native American, without any contact to the outer world. In contrast, the portrait of Wi-jún-jon is telling the alarming story of the consequences for Indians when encountering with the white-men's society.

Together with a few other Native Americans, Wi-jún-jon was invited to meet the president of the United States. On his departure in autumn 1831 he was 'dressed in his native costume, which was classic and exceedingly beautiful'[19]. On the left hand side of the Catlin's full-length portrait, he is clearly indigenous in appearance,

---

[16] Truettner, 82f.
[17] Ibid., 83f.
[18] Catlin, 'Letter-No. 49', 142.
[19] Ibid., 'Letter-No. 55', 222.

concerning the long leather tunic, leggings and moccasins, as well as the proudly unfolded long hair and the imposing ground-long headdress. The object in his hand is a wooden pipe. The figure is turned towards the left and thus displaying the strong profile features of a Native American. In the far backdrop lies the White House, which Wi-jún-jon is entering shortly to meet the head of state.

About half a year later, in which he had visited the achievements of civilisation, Wi-jún-jon returns to his tribe as the only survivor of the travelled group. On the way back, he is accompanied by Catlin, who is extremely amused by the 'metamorphose' and 'plight' of the Amerindian, which he describes as dressed in a blue military uniform and uncomfortable high boots, in which he is unable to walk properly; furthermore, he is wearing white gloves and holding redundant items, such as an umbrella and a fan.[20] The ridiculousness of his appearance is depicted in the right half of the painting, in which the figure of Wi-jún-jon is placed before tribal huts in the background and is facing away from the beholder. Truettner explains this as follows: 'The Light has become a swaggering dandy, a caricature of his former self, to whom he literally turns his back.'[21] Although the features and long hair reveal his ethnical identity, all other former attributes have been replaced by the redundant ones listed in Catlin's letter. By way of caution he added a cigarette and a bottle of alcohol, both signs of the Native American's moral decay.

Additionally, the artist informs the reader about the sad fate of Wi-jún-jon. According to him, the tribe believed that his experiences were fictitious, which greatly diminished his reputation. The souvenirs he brought were of no use to his people and thus converted into native clothing. Ultimately, he was even shot by one of his peers.[22]

Catlin's painting therefore needs to be understood as a warning. Wi-jún-jon had taken up vices of white society, yet he could not authentically adapt to civilisation, but became a laughing-stock instead. On the other side, he fell into the tribe's disgrace and was killed by his own people. The artist is presupposing that Native Americans cannot become part of the civilised world. The only choice they have is to remain in their natural territory and to continue living their 'pure' life in nature. Therefore, he once more affirms the belief in the lost, 'noble Indian'. Thinking one step further, by

---

[20] Ibid., 223.
[21] Truettner, 116.
[22] Catlin, 'Letter-No. 55', 223-227.

accepting this idea without attempting to make a change, George Catlin might even have contributed to the extinction of the remaining Native Americans.

Conclusion

Based on the preceding analysis, it becomes obvious that George Catlin carefully studied his subjects, their status in tribal hierarchy and their customs. Consequently, his portraits depict the individual characteristics of the sitter on canvas while, simultaneously, they are manipulated to convey a message related to the *zeitgeist*. Therefore, the paintings cannot be understood as naturalistic reproductions of Native Americans. Nevertheless, Catlin's paintings are a great contribution to the history of art, for they are influenced by history and thus visual documents of the culture in which they are embedded, as well as romantic memorials of their subjects. Especially the visual means used to represent and remember Native Americans are George Catlin's legacy to the canon of history of art.

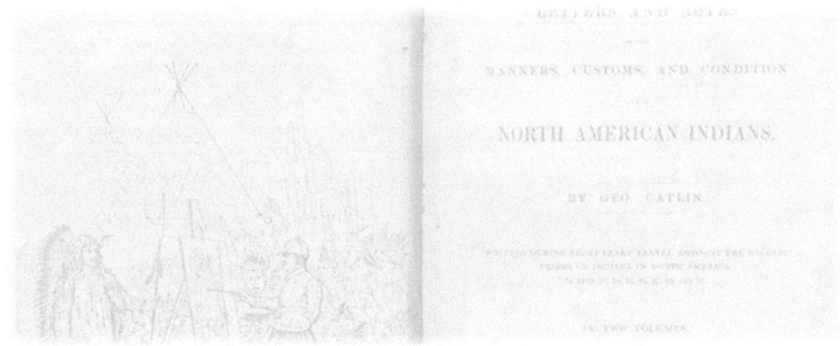

Bibliography

- ❖ Catlin, G., *Letters and Notes on the North American Indians*, Volume I and II, Dighton, Massachusetts, 1995.

- ❖ Groseclose, B., *Nineteenth-Century American Art,* Oxford, 2000.

- ❖ Knowles, S., 'Lecture 1: 'Introduction', in: *HA 2009: Creator and Subject,* UCC, 16.09.16.

- ❖ Nerburn, K., ed., *The Wisdom of the Native Americans*, Novato, California, 1999.

- ❖ Pohl, F., 'Old World, New World: the Encounter of Cultures on the American Frontier', in: S. Eisenman, *Nineteenth Century Art; A Critical History.* London, 1994.

- ❖ Truettner, William H. *Painting Indians and Building Empires in North America 1710-1840,* California, 2010.

List of Figures

Fig. 1

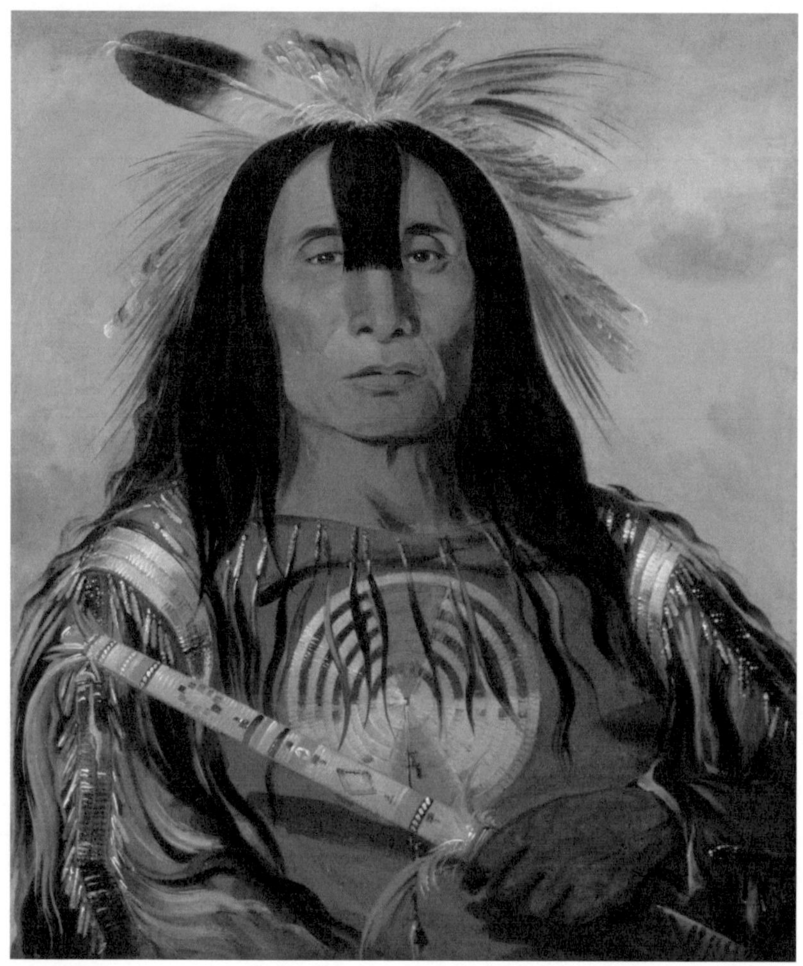

Fig. 2

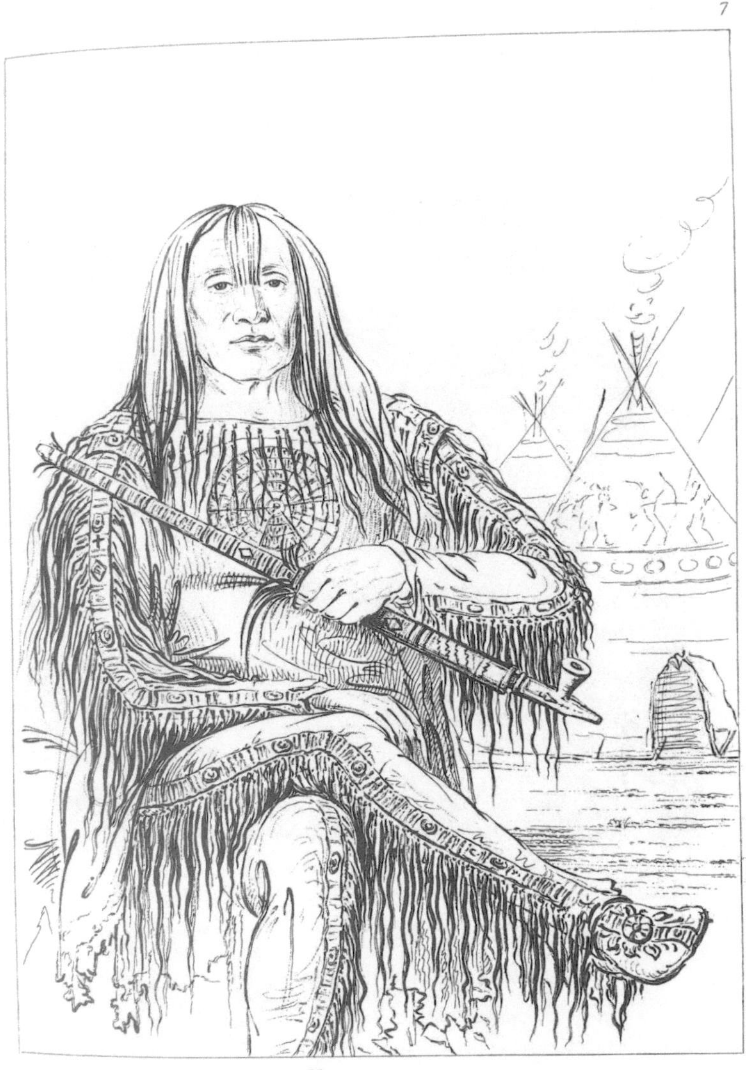

11

Fig. 3

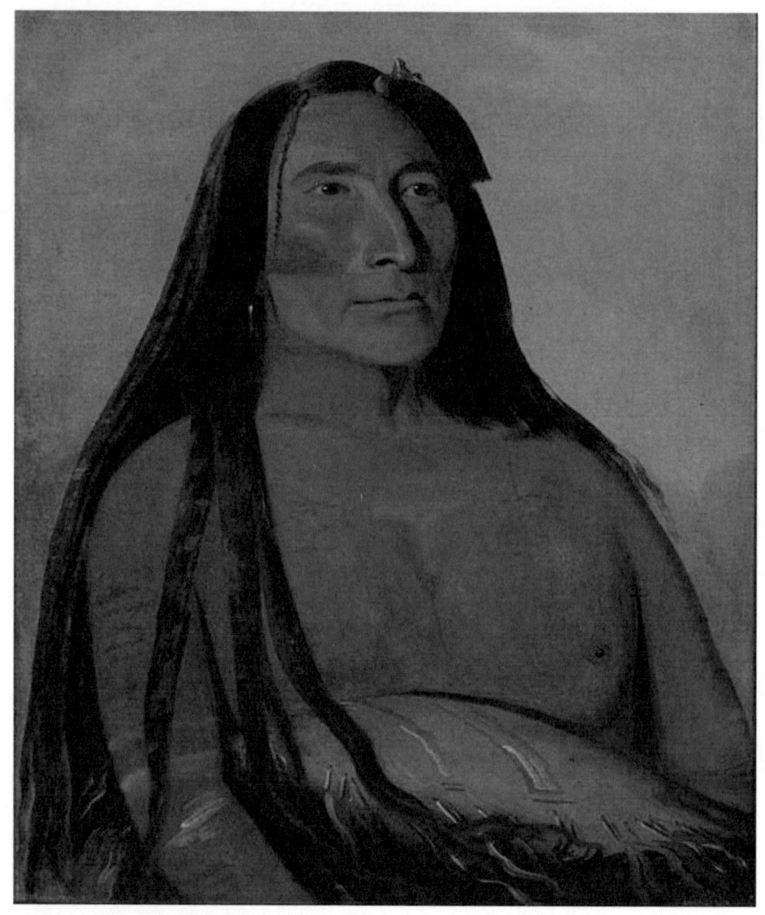

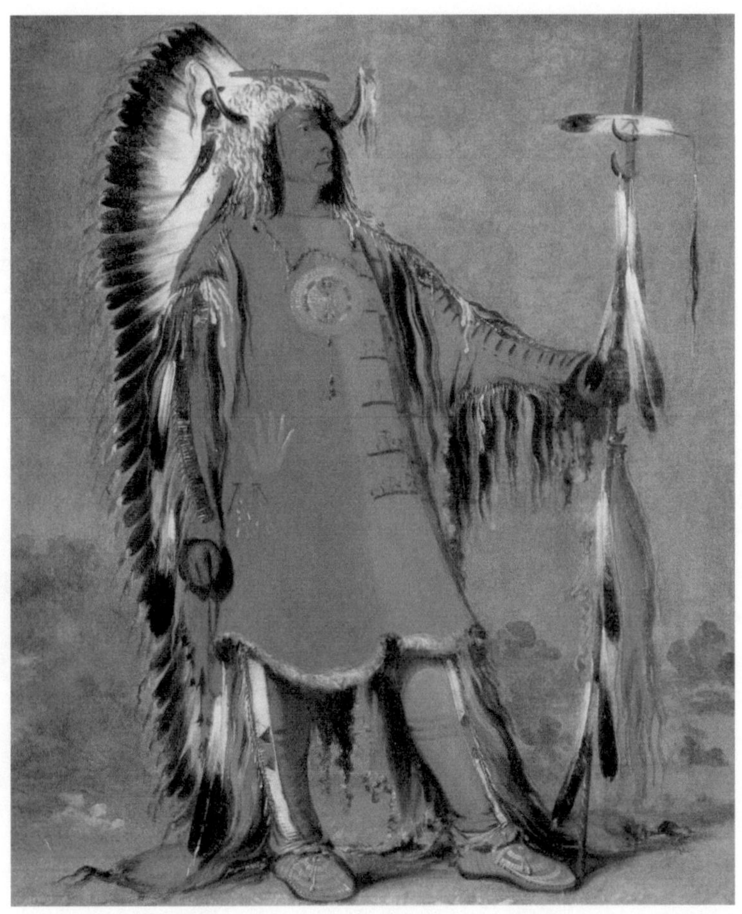

Fig. 5

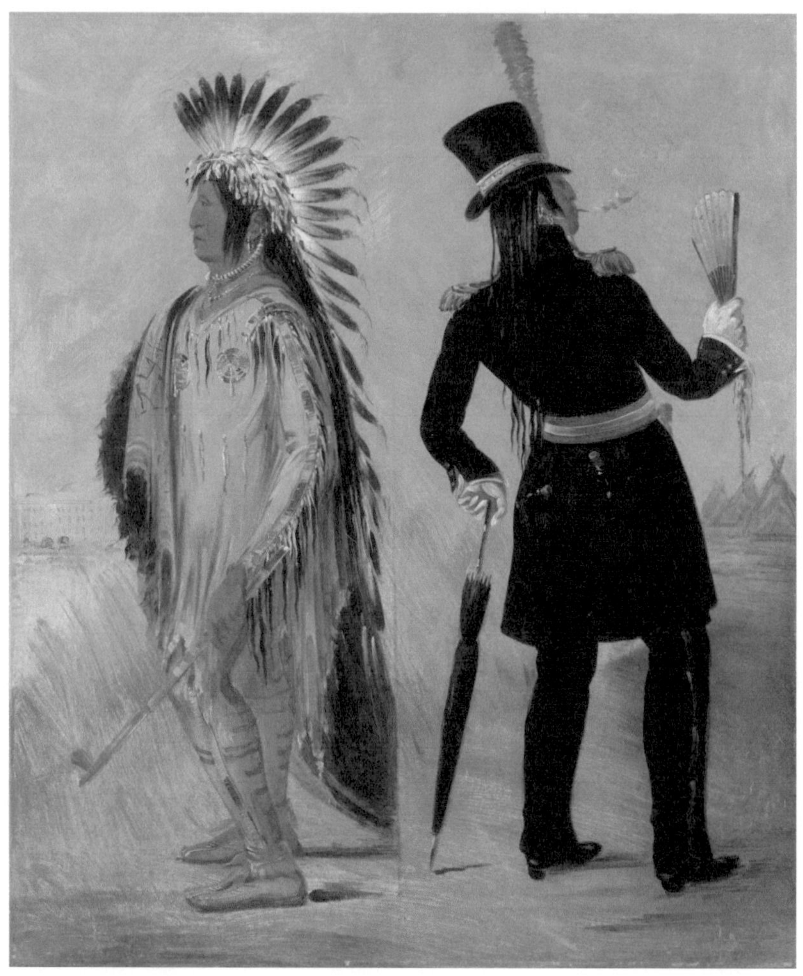

YOUR KNOWLEDGE HAS VALUE

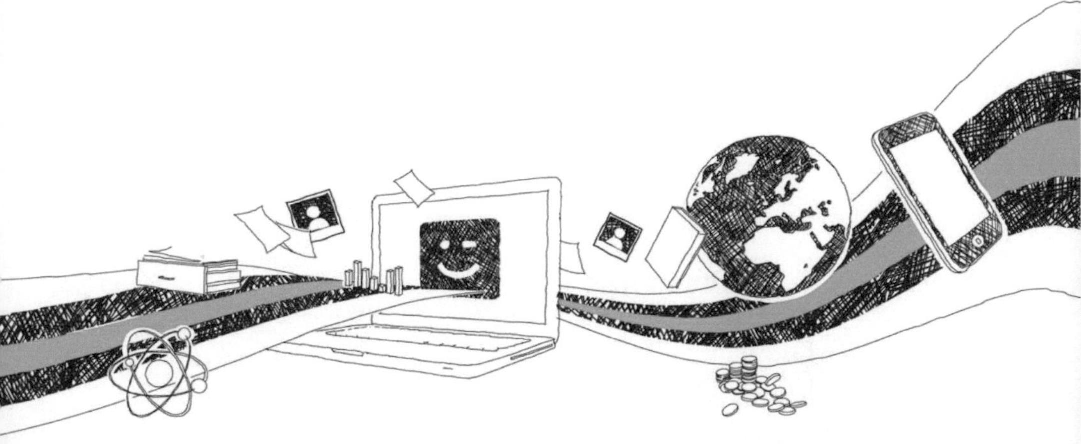

- We will publish your bachelor's and master's thesis, essays and papers

- Your own eBook and book - sold worldwide in all relevant shops

- Earn money with each sale

Upload your text at www.GRIN.com and publish for free

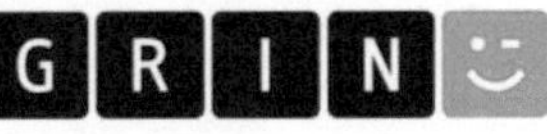